By Adrien Stoutenburg

HEROES, ADVISE US
SHORT HISTORY OF THE FUR TRADE

Greenwich
Mean
Time

Adrien
Stoutenburg

University of Utah Press
Salt Lake City
1979

For David R. Slavitt

Contents

Interiors I

Structures

These knobs, these minor huts
(a tiny company town)
lodged in a row beneath my skin
are the knuckles of my living hand
on which my right reach
and my grasp depend.

And these attendant shapes
strung out like rays
toward my deep pulse
(almost a crow's-foot-game
tricked out of common twine)
are tempted into strings and flutes
and hammer-strikes where,
on the soft side of my wrist,
a blue piano plays.

These are the stirrups of my feet,
the spur and arch that carry me
through blowing streets and days
toward nights as brittle as an aphid's lip.

The dunce caps where my thighs begin or end
are my strict knees that bend
in one direction only —
prayer or love.

These are my ribs,
this curved stockade around my breath,
a creaking circus ring
where shadow-shapes perform:
sad dwarfs on stilts,
contortionists, pale clowns,
and tumblers in a blare of silk

timing their antics to a drum.

And this, below, where body forks
like a mandrake root
is the inflexible frame
above the narrow locks
of pubic bones — those grudging gates
between delivery and death
that barely give, even in birth.
Just there the whirl comes down
from thorax, phalanges, salty spine,
and that red magistrate
where the sternum lifts
its guardian altar like a sword.

Maxilla, sacrum, sockets, nails,
and my round skull
(that high loft packed with brine
and want and wind) . . .
this is my skeleton entire,
a scaffold in its brittle sleeves
designed to bear the whining weight
of breath and gut and flesh,
but not regret's insistent tooth
nor the marrow ache of unspent love.

Anywhere

Within this inmost state
where the snail lives curled
and the turtle schemes under his green roof
and the spider knits like a grandmother —
    within this web, this dark,
    this woven spell, self-woven,
    nothing is complete
    for all its tight, curved inwardness.

The sky hangs over all
    and is flash or gray as it wills.
The wind hunts under all
    and is fierce or sweet as it chooses.
The sun still rises —
    how it charges my sleeping eyelids —
and falls. Somewhere it is drunk in the sea.
    Here it impales itself on mountains
wearing snow like a new, white forest.

I am alone in this inmost state
but surrounded by the quick, insouciant grass,
and by young trees with the sense to try to live.
    My desk is with me, and some books.
    My breath remains. I am using it
    in an inward, outward way
    for some unknown purpose.
The inmost thing, within, locked like a knife,
is not breath, is not heart is . . .

    a knot in the bone, a knuckle in the chest,
    a sense of great distances
    that cannot be vaulted, being too blue,
    the air too rare.
                Something spins there

if not in me. Something glides
into the dream of a dream.
    But that is outer, outward, beyond.

The snail, curled like a gray finger,
is resident here
and its cheek is damp.
The spider keeps a dry workroom.
The turtle is in love with fish.
    We live together in harmony,
    ignoring the birds
    in the country far beyond us.

The Sleep of Animals

There is no way to enter into it.
They are enclosed, infolded,
rolled deep in their own darkness.
There is no way to follow their visions,
neither those of the horse, the sloth, the tiger,
not even the household mascot.
Only by a quiver of a haunch,
a twitch of an ear or whisker,
or sometimes the white of an eye rolling
can one guess that they dream at all.

I shall never know
what perfumed field the pony grazed,
what hammock the sloth invented,
what orange memories fed the tiger;
nor they
what jungles I explore,
what hearts I savor,
in my own night,
as deep as any.

Night Cabin

In winter no man knows his friend;
    great bears like windy haystacks come
    out of a forest sleep to drum
    with midnight knuckles on a door.
Who knows what such hot brutes intend,
    hearing, within, a carol of bees?

Whatever knocks on night or breathes —
    a weasel's tooth, a branch, a wing
    spun from the cold — his listening
    ear invents a neighbor he can love.
A tame wind nickers and the eaves
    seem safe with stars, assuaging doubt.

At some steep hour he will go out
    and lead inside the thing he feared,
    then sit with it, blind to the beard
    that weaves a shadow for that face
(the eyes too small, the nose a snout)
    immune to love, and honey-smeared.

Dogskin Rug

Second grade mornings
it held some warmth for my waking feet
in its deep, collie-colored hair,
even when the rainspout froze
to a cataract gray
and winter gasped beneath
the December floor.

Only he, sprawled headless,
was a carpet there,
with a short flash of tail;
bright white it wagged
on a backyard line
when my grandmother's rug-beater throbbed
dust back into an antic life.

He had been a playmate of my infancy,
she said, and too much loved
to toss back to the bone-heaped world.

Beneath the fur
there was the skin
lean as parchment
with a leaf-map of veins.
At times I dreamed a heart
still drumming there,
or a crib of teeth
around an indolent, summer bone;
as under a buffalo robe
in the old, flapping car,
I thought of windy beards
and hoofs.
               Coonskin or pony's pelt,
we borrowed their warmth

for days when cold creaked
like a ship, the world as bare
as their lost skeletons.

I was content
on those sharp days and nights,
alone,
to have that speechless collie there.

Cellar

That time I tumbled into the dark —
   tilt, plunge, and cry
   through a trap door left open
   in a trusted pantry floor —

      that descent, child-hair streaming,
      into a kingdom of potatoes
      (their tall eyes sprouting upward
      like pale rockets),
      dried onions, squash, cold fists of cabbages,
      carrots hanging like withered darts,
      preserves and relish winking
      from provident shelves,
but the dust alive and daintily clawed:

      that moment of plunging through linoleum
      embossed with faded birds
      (the bitter smell of wind
      or coal or something darker
      hunched inside a box),
      the gasp of arrival on hardened earth,
      then the quick leap up
      the raw wood stairs
      toward a living room with lights still on —
        being saved from rot
        and breathing mice
        and the crimson stars of tomatoes sliced
      and staring out of glass —
resurrected, full of heart . . .

      but now on deeper nights
      a different void
      below the humpbacked dreams,
      and no light left

except a clock's dim hands
that pace my gray,
yet climbing, breath.

Country School

When we walked through winter
our lunch pails hummed with apples.
Each round lid kept
a spotted windfall in,
high company for bread.

At noon, winesaps and russets
spilled an orchard's breath.
I thought of great, hot, chiming boughs,
and saved the sweetness for the last.

The cloakroom sent
fragrance of rubbers, ice, and wool.
In the brown stove the fire cracked.
The hour thinned.
I ate my apple
and the white core leaked
its gray perfume of tin.

A Winter View

In such blind weather,
    trees and sky sagging with rain,
clouds out of harness
    romping from sheen to blackness
to pastures of long sleet,
    I used to draw at the round kitchen table.
The lamp was there,
    dropping its oval of false sunlight,
while darkness and wind
    peered around corners,
and frost began to grave
    white manes of horses on the window.

Rain has no odor, only what it borrows
    from grass or dust
or the very blue bins of memory.
    Frost is a different guest.
It is the coldest of flowers.
It is the whitest of scents.
It is a gathering of jewels,
    formal as a bouquet,
    but subject to change by a fingernail.

My awe was keen, but not enough
    to leave those fantasies
    between me and a further view.
    Some extra vision was required,
    and my hot breath,
    round as a pond,
worked like a torch.

    I breathed, I breathed,
    in order to see through.

Hypochondria

There is always dread that the disease,
    unnamed as yet,
will escape our vigil. The twitch in the night —
    a fork turning —
the tug in the cave of the heart,
    the giddiness without reason,
the sense of falling and failing,
    even the exhilaration
just before the plumb-weight of fatigue
    hauls down, and breath dangles
at the edge of the edge —
    all the blue meadows of the past
running off with their live shadows,
    birds broken,
winds bruised beyond recognition,
    mementos (whole albums of flowers, soft hair,
and the light on faces)
    tossed out with leaves
for the annual burning.

Morning rituals are required:
    investigation of the sudden blemish;
a cyst, unwarranted, beside an ear;
    a knot in heel or groin,
an itch, a pang,
    a narrow drumbeat in the bone
where deep beyond the X-ray hides
    an unoriginal but nervous sin.

There is always dread that the disease,
    if left unmonitored,
might turn into some common thing —
    a simple wart, heat rash, a fading bruise —
and leave us unprepared to bear

the knife within
that like a red key turns
to expose the inner void,
inoperable as love,
and as deadly as despair.

The Rink

Hell has not frozen
but trains its blowtorches
on every sunset.
It will never confine
its huge kingdom to any country,
stoked by all winds and wills,
nor will it congeal,
form a cold river
for us to frolic on
with our bladed conscience skimming
over pearl patterns
or fish turned white.

Look down through the false ice
a lying winter has invented,
and observe the busy furnace
just where the rink seems
most solidly silver.

Hans Brinker never dreamed of that abyss.
His runners were truer than ours,
still innocent,
and the canal was sound.

How different it is to skate on fire.

Message

Something has caught in my throat,
neither frog nor bone,
more like a fork
that tastes of alum,
or a stone that has lived in fire,
possibly a jewel
(the ruby's red glass furnace),
perhaps a diamond, unpolished
(white eye in darkness),
or simply my own breath
grown jagged,
trapped between speech and silence.

There is no surgeon for this,
or not one near enough
this high-pitched place
whirled round by mountains
and the wind's unfettered voice.

I shall learn sign language
but even then the stone
or fork or fire, desire's impediment,
will make my hands stutter.

Consider this when next I call
or try to signal
across mesas, thunder, gulfs,
and the garrulous crosses
of telephone poles.

Evening might be the best time,
when I am a silhouette —
or some deep morning
when, in stillness,

you could catch the beat —
the clear and strenuous tone —
of that fixed voice
where my heart swings
in its round perch,
alone, yet not alone.

As It Is

for Laura

Wife love, father love, love of an old dog,
whatever love it is — if it is love —
is twined through stress
(disease, a wound, a grinding debt)
into so tight a skein
the leanest filament seems gross:
    threads in light bulbs;
    split ends of human hair;
    the close, red conduits
    through which blood creaks and booms
    in echo chambers of motels,
    deserted chairs, black trains,
    or just a dusty seashell in a drawer,
    curved like a porcelain ear.

Things shake and sigh with it —
roofs, knobs, and doors —
and common neighbors coming home,
seeing an ambulance,
a wandering child,
a foreign license plate,
an empty yard,
or furniture stacked outside
like varnished bones.

It toils and sleeps;
it wrestles and cooks meals,
copes with mountains, dust cloths, tears;
carries out trash, seeks interviews,
limps through heat; scrubs, burrows, cries,
boils water, holds a dying paw,
        does what it does

to keep pain back awhile — if it is pain —
as it must be
if it is love.

Portraits **II**

f/16, 1/500

When you go again into the heartland
with its known temples, dance halls, bogs —
travel light except for that third eye
that stares from behind its monocle,
then blinks to capture what is there.
It may hold, better than your mind,
the match-quick nerves that flare
across a stiffly focused smile,
or catch the unseen worm at work
in a wave of living hair.

Some passerby in that same land
may press a sunburned thumb
and record you, in turn,
upon the winding reel
that winks your image out of time
toward colored forgeries that keep
even the sweat, a constant rim,
around your own unshuttered eyes.

2.
The trick of resurrection lies
in darkroom skills, a proper blend
of heat and cold, of acids made to lift
the buried image into day — though not until
all shadows, gleams, are fixed,
the worm developed and made clear.

One errant ray distorts and slays:
two lovers on a simple road
become two ghosts, mouth pressed
to blurred and bitter mouth,
exposed beyond reprieve, a faceless pair
hung on a drying rack, head down,

out of the luminous air.

Beware of too much light,
whatever kind;
but, most, the headlong flash
of truth
that burns all fake scenarios
(like yours and mine)
to albums of instant ash.

From the Diggings

In 1919, archeologists digging among grave mounds
along an ancient Roman road in Luxembourg
discovered a crystal phial containing tears shed
two thousand years before.

The dust is known and filled with teeth,
dead hairpins, urns, a breastplate scabbed
by preening rot. In the hot drift
the trowels burn, and picks, long-eyed as pelicans,
chip through the dark,
unearthing common things
until, just where the grave swell ends —
a gleam. A wink. A something caught
and stoppered up like rain;
salt, grief, and residue intact.

No burgomaster, serf, or slave,
not even a huntsman trimmed in fur,
possessed such dainty sepulchres.
    Some queen with sodden lids
    preserved her pain
    in that slim vault;
    some melancholy prince —
    unless upon one desperate night
    a jester stole into his monarch's room
    and, armed with crystal, teased a royal ape
    until that clanking beast, like any king,
    wept from his tiny, blood-swept eyes.

Ivory Paper Weight

Elephants are born with so much clothing,
wrinkled and folded,
and such a cargo of bones, cartilage, nerves —
only their brains being small, gray jewels —
and everyone a Cyrano,
noses curled like vines,
but tuskless, the sucking mouths open.

The cow has two breasts only,
a kind of mountainous woman
on tree trunk legs,
and a body wide enough
to create shade without leaves.
The young one stands there
as under a parasol of rock.

Bulls keep to themselves
after rutting;
sometimes go mad
from a strange gland in the forehead,
or an abscessed wound;
are massive, always,
twice-ponderous in rage or lust.

That one I held in my thought . . .
that one, older than the hunters who stung him,
forever walking backward to keep the wind
from his bullet-silvered eyes . . .

I searched for him through circuses and dream,
held his knobbed head
(a dying mountain, nerve-crossed as a leaf),
then touched a brittle tusk.
It shattered, traveled, and rolled down

to this blind figurine
that holds — at times —
the papers on my blowing desk,
and my beast-haunted mind.

Whales

They mate as we do,
bear their young alive,
feed them from nipples,
yet they breathe like fountains.

Their brains are small,
and hard to bring back in jars,
turning to slop from the ship's motion;
but their entrails shine, when fresh,
as softly tinted as coils of rainbows.

They exude oil like Texas.
Their bleached jawbones and ribs
make cathedrals on windy islands.
The strainers in baleen mouths
are a forest of hard gates
packed with moss,
misplaced beards clotted
with shrimp, plankton, and krill.

In the toothed whales
there are white spires
as ancient harpooners learned
whose skulls drift now
like pallid seeds
below the spouting shadow of
Leviathan.

Encounter

The shark's sad smile
was upsidedown
and he came through the water
like a spear of smoke
bending with each current
that roped him round
and swung him and was swung.
But his teeth were a forest
stripped of all leaves
and his eyes, deeper than stones,
were too sharply near.
I merely poked him in the snout
and he pouted off
like a hurt, though deadly, child.

Water Strider

This stranger on slanted legs
straddles an inch of water,
adjusts his pointed heels
and twirls upon his shadow;
for his shadow is always with him,
hanging from his belly,
its green face looking up
to his leaning face above it.
His other shadow, down deep,
hangs from the yellow sun
and lights up each blue foot,
flat in a whirling sandal.

Self-Portrait

In this sketch I am in a canoe
as silver as a young moon,
and the water is so still
it hums with the pickerel's delicate teeth.
The water is so deep
the sunfish's lantern burns out,
and my hook is a steel question mark
hanging upsidedown in all the night
the lake hauls to itself
from forests, scum, or passing rot.

I am wearing a white shirt,
the sleeves pushed up,
and at my feet a jug of wine rolls
like a round, glass child.
My tackle box is trim,
and a painted bobber winks
above the barb designed
to lure some hunger underneath.

It is all deceit —
the boat, the gaff hook, net, and knife,
props only for a chance to watch, alone,
the light and wind and perchless sky.
I dread the least tug at the line,
the gasping weight, the wounded throat,
but the risk of blood, as everywhere, is great.

Tulip Fancier

They are self-centered,
concentrated as knuckles,
lie stacked and sorted
like paper-wrapped skulls
in the bins beneath my house:
Darwins, Rembrandts, Mendels,
time-clocks inside them
whirring at their round, dry foreheads.

This one, in love with habit,
is determined to be pink
with a precise pathway of silver
on the tongue of each petal;
this one is concerned only
with orangeness and feathered edges.
That one, brooding in a corner,
is obsessed with becoming vermilion.

Even in the slow pendulum of summer,
out of their nests, there is a hum.
Something fanatic is there,
and the mouthless bulbs,
gorged with the fat of what was
stem and flower,
simmer with waiting.

Judgment Day

The slug was too near
the fire of weeds and old wood,
a low, bullet-shaped thing,
his invisible gut
pink with my choice begonias.

Still, I lifted him,
gray turd of life,
and tossed him toward salvation,
though it will earn me no points
when my red turn comes.

Conflagrations

At night, late enough for prayers,
I saw the old man here,
a peripheral relative
with nowhere but my pagan flat to go,
kneel in his shift,
chin bent against his steeped hands.

His feet like dirty mushrooms peeked
from underneath his gown.
I added an ice cube to my drink
and listened to thunder in the streets
where traffic traveled up and down,
and crickets drove dark nail on nail.

His sins, he daily confessed, or bragged,
were as black as the wig upon his skull;
he preached of judgment at any hour,
when God's steepest angels, whirling spears
(their own nightshirts in flame),
would descend upon the wicked world
(and such as me
who would not plead or bow)
with vengeance in their soaring hair.

At blind midnight, he snored
upon his borrowed bed,
while I lay wakeful, unredeemed.

I heard the dripping tap,
a rock band's manic beat next door,
and then the sirens, louder than harps,
wailing toward some neighbor's
suddenly crimson home —
and prayed for them, and firemen
with hoses, swift, and perfectly aimed.

V.D. Clinic

How bald that microscope was,
    eye without lashes
    except for my student gaze
    fringed at the peephole
    where pale, swimming commas arrived
    on the stage,
    trapped on a slide
    as naked as a mirror.

A woman had been surprised,
the smear alive
with the richness of a recent lover.
    Positive Wasserman; positive guilt.
    My starch coat creaked and turned.

Her legs were thin.
Her stockings hung.
Her eyes were not,
had never been her own.

A sting of medicines,
    a scent as from the mouth
        of someone chewing herbs —
            and something clanged:

the waste can's lid
above the swabs . . .
    and then the noiseless skid
        of beasts or angels skating down
            into their nameless, cotton graves.

Solo, Non-Stop

Donald Crowhurst set out from England in 1968
to sail non-stop around the world. His radio
messages told of a record-smashing voyage before
his boat was found adrift, empty, in mid-ocean.
He had been sailing in circles for eight months
when apparently he threw himself into the sea.

My lie was my gift
made out of lost stars
and a circling ghost of shores
never reached.

My boat, too, was false,
warped and fragile from the start,
a brittle pod
consumed by spray
and waves greener than hills,
while my compass needle spun
like devil-dust,

But
think of my messages
to you snug at home —
signals of a hero
wrapped in sharks and thunder,
pursuing always
the prize that jigged
beyond your safe, slow meadows —

each of you sustained,
sailing imaginary oceans,
ever achieving
in my spendthrift shadow:

smashers of records,

dreamers, inheritors of islands
and headlines,
    smoking pipes in your bedrooms,
    waiting in the underground,
    or dressing for dinner,
    safe from my skull's blue drowning.

The Brotherhood

They are there at the bar, singing, all of them,
except those who crashed, full of blood
and Irish coffee, or whose hearts stopped,
stumbling up roads too steep for breath.
They are all friends there, blazing in brotherhood
even when they are strangers without names,
or with last names only — Peterson, Schmidt,
Manolini, O'Brien — or are trapped in labels —
the Wino, the Widow, the Nervous Wreck, the Preacher —
singing together at midnight, or at dawn weeping
at frog faces swimming into a mirror.

One thing they all know — even the Wino knew
before he was buried with his round earring shining
like an old wedding band — is what they are there for:
not to be caught alive alone; not to be dead alone;
not to be too far, sober on a cold street,
from the Bartender or the Seaman or even the Nervous Wreck
rattling between the oil stove and the door,
his neck in flight from his long, bird's shoulders,
even the Woman-in-the-walker who has ceased singing
but who listens, almost alone in the other room,
the room itself dead now, a big casket
where the fire smokes and the parrot burns green
and yells, loud as torn metal,
"Have another! Have another! On me!"

"A mean bird," the Bartender says.
"It hates people." He opens early
for the sake of the red-eyed, shaking boys
who blazed too long the night before.
All day he limps behind the bar
that is brown with breath and booze and age,
while the hills rise up around him toward

a sky consumed by wind-drunk trees.

His lead foot drags. One eye is cocked
toward what he is not looking at;
you can't be sure which eye is watching you.
"I was born dead," he says with pride.
Somebody, God or aunt, blew life through him
and put him in an oven to keep warm.
He still has his first diaper, and brags,
"This big," he says, and makes a triangle
like a church's cupola with clean forefingers
and black-thatched thumbs.
The wall clock watches with one eye,
uncrippled, sly.

       Dark hair is touched with white,
       and lines are working down the faces there,
       invisible at night. Only the parrot hates.
       The rest are wild and loud with love.

Aging Acrobat

The arena of choice narrows to a tightrope
thinner than a saw,
and, below, faces of past performers float
like flecks of sawdust in the abyss
where all must tumble, in time,
with or without decision.

To keep one's poise
a day or a year longer,
to teeter in space
while leaning against the wind
(clinging to a vision
or to a common balance pole
that even clowns can use),
it is essential to select
the right step at the right moment;
and then, if falling, with no net left,
or all nets rotten,
even then to attempt some grace
in that untutored plunge
into simplicity.

Headhunter

His mother's skull
nods on his chest,
an eyeless pendulum
protecting him from the bitter ghosts
of those whose heads
he hacked and cured
to save his own.

Such trophies, once salvation, lie
beyond his reach, except in dream,
since the new fathers came
in their black coats and shoes,
their crucifix more powerful
than pig tusks wreathing his dark wrists.

Forbidden now the manhood rites —
the drumming, dugout voyage
through bullrushes and drowsy birds,
the deep-grass-taste of night
when as a child initiate
he played at death,
drank down a kinsman's blood
and was reborn.

Restraint is thin, the chapel bleak,
but with these come tobacco,
penicillin, grace, the promise of redemption,
and immortal life.

Still, all must watch
the shadow of old bones,
touch amulets, make secret chants,
since no one can be sure
that just behind the ceremonial cave

or cross
some resurrected shade may not arrive
in immaculate robe and flesh,
hair haloed by the sun,
his arm upraised — forgiving none.

Fashion Model at Home

Every night he waits at the window
    with the gun,
and every night I pretend
    he is not there,
and do my nails as usual,
    hang my nylons from the shower rod,
and brush my teeth
    to prevent decay, bad breath, and death,
and set my hair.

I graze the mirror with a glance
    for fear of seeing him
over my shoulder
    and his naked smile.
All windows I keep locked,
    for the winds, when hot,
carry his groundhog smell;
    in winter, an ice pick enters
with his stare.

He will tunnel in some day,
    or blast his way —
    a vein exploding,
    a trap door pried.
When the gun goes off,
    someone else will have to attend
to my eyes, my mouth
    (stitching it back to something more in style),
and my easy-to-care-for hair.

True Crime

Who did it? Not the butler.
Not even the weak son
riding at polo, his tunic green
to match the money from the will.
Not the sly cook, either,
nor the old dog dozing
beside an empty limousine.

It was the clock, the way it paced
midnight and dawn,
the cocktail hour,
schedules of buses, trains,
arrivals on the moon,
the moment when bank doors
would let him in or lock him out,
the traffic signal's red and green,
the instant of some sudden vision
instantly passed into the past.

It was the clock,
the days it metered out —
each day with the same clanging face —
and seasons chained to ancient ways.

He had a sense of his own pace.
No clock was geared to time the rush
of bullet to brain
or just how long a breath he took
before the final tick and gong.

Rest Home

Each year, the mirror wrinkles,
and the leaves fall, each fall,
more swiftly than they ever came.
The rain is rinsed of blueness,
is merely falling gray
against which the chill, bent old
wear their galoshes zipped,
or brood indoors.
              The wheelchairs whine
like power lines in a blizzard wind.
Checkerboards click. See the hand
that's moving there,
its bones concealed a bit
by withering spurs of flesh and hair.

They plod and nod, stammer at prayer,
are shaved by dutiful volunteers,
slump with bitten nails outstretched
for tints of red or Mandarin orange.
The alert yearn for a bridge,
a rope, a knife.
The stubborn dead are busy shuffling cards.

Iowa Biography

for Josie

The horizon was hers beyond the barn
and running fields. Heaven, assured,
hung where the church spire reached
to hold up half the stretching sky
above stork-regiments of corn.
Yet, something underfoot and ripe —
ground cherries, squash, red gift of fallen plums —
gave faith an extra nourishment
and her wide, working hands
a chance to reverence earthy things:
chicks yellower than dandelions,
roundness of apples and Mason jars,
milk pails, loud churns — and bread:
almost it seemed, each time,
Christ newly risen
out of yeast's strange coils and springs,
essential miracle for child and child
shouting across the crowded wind.

Those shouts had an eager way of going,
though echoes clung to porch and swing.
Earth, in age, brought different sounds.
The windmill gasped that turned the air
through eighty years of days.
Corn was louder, darker, at dusk,
then changed to just a dream of sound
in a rented room where silence grew,
and only the clock knew a cricket tune.

Ghosts thumped white fists on the waiting door;
lost bones of chicks or children blew
on a siren's wail. Against some living visitor,

blizzards spun wagons of unwanted lace,
and pain kept time with her tatting hands.

Still, roots with keen inverted spires
thrust down to hold the world awhile.
Horizons dimmed to a waning clock
on the dresser where rose-scented beads
dozed within drawers beside chocolate hearts,
a fading garden of photographs,
holiday cards wrinkled like husks,
a Bible, trinkets, a ball of twine —
harvest, oh, harvest, harvest!

Landscapes

Stopover: Iceland

Cod is the savior of this land,
hanging like gray sleeves from drying racks,
stuffed headless into salt-cold barrels
while children train in thermal pools,
mouths blue as gills
beneath their shivering hair.

The guide extolls the moderate air,
the lack of pain or crime,
the independence of the soul,
the literate mind, the Althing's care
for men and trees —
though few branched things are there,
and dogs in Reykjavik are banned.

Bronze-eyed, a metal pack horse stares
through blizzards in the city square,
the sculptured saddlebags no heavier
than those the living beast lugged out
across the landscape's wrinkled scabs,
heaps and hell-forms, boulders, slags,
debris of giants' fists and thighs,
volcanic rot and buried fire.

The land has never aimed toward pine,
content to dream of twigs and moss —
or, at the most, dwarf birch and naked grass —
striving toward mountains, glaciers, birdless crags.

Eagles are rare. The polar bear
drifts in on floes, then leaves again,
white visitor on his white raft.
The snake is absent, like the frog,
and few things chime in pale spring nights,

except the rocks. Beside the highway's emptiness,
cairns stand like human forms,
rough torsos from some wandering wish of hands
to impress shape upon the stone-mad fields.

Book stalls and churches help the fault,
and the welfare state is lenient.
Against the tremors and deep flames,
concrete cooperatives
defy the shock of daily breath.
But, still, beneath all things —
the kindergarten pool and desk,
the fish-strung rack, the tourist bus —
the rocks build up, and wait.

Drumcliffe: Passing By

Cast a cold Eye
On Life, on Death.
Horseman, pass by!
  — W. B. Yeats's tombstone

It was rain and green and always rain,
and the May cold spilling through rock walls
into bone-walls and breath, caught in the folds
of clothing and breath, dripping where farmers walked
like swimmers trapped in weedy boots,
hissing on hedges and dogs and death.
Rain has its home there, building ditches, ruins,
and green-haired wives.
                              At Yeats's grave,
under a black umbrella's roof,
I understand how rarely blue exists
and how, no doubt, his poet's skull
lies packed with moss in less than thirty years
beneath his plain, admonishing stone.

The rooks were noisy rags in blowing trees.
Swallows, as neat as bats, dived through mist
for their winged food.
                        No horseman I,
but still a rider through rain and green
and dusk, casting a cold eye.

San Andreas City: For Active Adults

The fault, named for a saint,
is snakelike in design,
twisting through slums and campuses
and leisure worlds: a gut, a void,
a braid of thunder,
a dreamer in a slit, brown mask.

It lisps below all lives,
even in this protracted scheme
where guards patrol bridge games and sleep,
and golf greens click like a chorus of tacks.

The stucco hills remain unmoved as yet.
The swimmers drift through chlorinated calm
or float with highballs balanced on their hearts
while "The Blue Danube," amplified,
drowns out the tick beneath their breath,
and beach balls nodding like human heads
obscure the crack (though deepening)
below the diving board's agile wrist.

Shore Leave: Provincetown

The sleepless buoy, all night,
ruins my own sleep:
mechanical loon or lunatic,
night watchman manacled to the sea,
intoning with moan and chime to me
(and to you — you silent beside me here),
"Beware, beware,
all you who seek to rest
on water or, at such steep midnights,
anywhere."

Some hurt seems fastened there
in the flat foam,
stitched to a trawler's hull,
stuck in a wet gull's throat,
and here; nailed into beach hotels
like ours
where tourist faces gasp in fog
and long for hills, hot fields,
even some brittle desert home;

all, all of us here
driven by the incessant chant,
then driven in turn
to shops and bars,
a kaleidoscope of galleries,
pool tables, passionate indoor games,
while motorcycles wilder than guns
add their cacophony
to the sailors' metronome
where rocks are supposed to be.

Here in this night,
within this drift, this bed,

with you beside me, silent,
knowing there is nothing more
for us, not anywhere, no more to be said,
I hear a different buoy intone
what those in perilous harbors
learned before,
"Take care, take care,
the dangers are on shore."

Art Colony by the Sea

Martinis seem soaked in weed;
kelp arrives like a ghost in all glasses,
and the starfish, alive,
looks up from the cognac snifter.
Everywhere, the sea's mildew clings and conquers,
rusts on iron, molds on easels.

The whole affair sinks into sadness
and a discussion when the fog slides in
as it always does at dusk and morning,
of how the dodgers or the giants are doing.
Who has won? Who has a chance of winning?

Point of View

Our first day there
the rain indoors
hissed in pans,
dropped hammers in kettles,
planned ruinous lakes
around each treasure
the moving van had left.

I carried long buckets
of tar and anger
up to the roof,
hunted blue serpents,
suspected whales swimming
under the shingles —
found harp-strings and choirs,
birds folded on branches
like gloves,
eaves running with ribbons,
leaves turned into mirrors —
sat back on my haunches
and marveled:
rain outside
is so different a matter.

Deluge

There is weather to come,
to live through,
everything we prize
clutched under our armpits,
and what gunpowder we have,
secured in our long hair.

I see our bones rising like white branches.
I see our many hearts, floating upward,
assembled into cold, red islands.

I hear, far off, the cry of rabbits drowning,
elephants sinking like anchors,
typewriters tapping under moss,
trains stopping, blinded by fish.

Even now, our bandtail pigeons fly
ever higher. There is rage in the creek,
the bays, the ocean,
and the false rainbow reflects its bridge
in a meadow of broken bottles.
The beaks of all birds are as thin as sandpaper;
the waters are already loud
with the lament of arks sinking.

Summer

The sorrow of small towns in summer,
the stillness of store windows,
the sun building a nest under awnings,
the scorch-smell of tomato vines and aprons,
the look of the park hunched,
awaiting the hope of evening;
the cottonwoods as quiet as cauliflowers,
the porches snoring with old men and dogs;
children white-haired from the drift of dandelions . . .

the train going by in black sweat,
and the rubber whine of the highway
where hurtling strangers pursue
the phantom of a lake on the pavement . . .

the gasp of carp in a river of tires,
and the long sigh of people walking
over trestles or under clotheslines;
the throb of flies in the post office,
the yelp of the noontime whistle,
the hard hum of roller skates
as the heat lightning shudders
and the great cyclone green of the sky
makes every face glimmer
like paste under water . . .

the swirl at the heart of the vacuum,
shirts blowing and the shutters fastened,
the stir of dust on Bible and trinket,
the dry lisp in the gutters,
the flash and false joy of sprinklers . . .

the sudden longing for the sorrow of winter.

Waste

Old houses, old bones
    (and a young cat dead
    on the highway,
    like sleep surrounded
    by golden stripes),
    or the hand of one leaf
    riding a gutter —
    palm yellow and shriveled —
all things abandoned,
twisted, cast-off,
bring a taste of mildew,
a savor of brass, like dread;
    impossible to diagnose
    but having much to do
    with old houses, old raptures,
    even rubbish cans
    stuffed with last year's news.

I begin to fear the journey
    in spite of golfers along the way,
    or a waltzing colt
    with a mane like a shock of black wind,
    or lovers loitering in each other's gaze.

My own house seems firm
    yet even here
    I catch at times
    a brittle gasp
    as of old sorrows, letters, loves,
    part of my own life's trash
    and buried deep,
    though not so deep
    some rummaging wind
    (of mind or mood or dream)

cannot haul them out
and hang them high in all their rags.

The sanitation trucks,
    stuffed with cargoes of dead cats,
    ruined golf clubs, halters, leaves,
    roll by like hearses,
    indifferent to the ghosts
    that creak and sigh in my back yard.
There is no agency for these.

This Being the Evening

This being the evening of the day
when birds fly like memories of themselves,
and the trees' armpits are alive
with beetles, ants, the insistent moss
gathered like cloth on thighs of bark . . .

everyone will be here soon, singing,
their voices higher than clarinets.
Up in the hills the wheat goes mad.
Cats walk, slowly, over their own shadows,
and the daisies lean toward snow,
fringed, yellow-eyed, devouring the sun.

Sometimes I walk there
and find the edge of the rampant hill
against the blue face-edge of the sky.
Clouds have shapes of Michelangelo
together with the brick color of some sunsets
floating over water.

The noise of leaves brings dry guitars.
Yesterday we cut down a tree.
The stump looks at us now,
and I remember how a grave stood open,
with hills of corn behind it.
There was a barbed wire fence
stretching around the cemetery.
Cars went by, flapping and shining,
while the hearse stood still,
a dignified driver smoking behind the wheel.

Dust

        is a force, a father,
a fellow traveler
(here, there, where you are),
bent under a gray load
but lugging it forever forward,
filling up hour-glasses,
smudging the wind's forehead,
prying into trunks and pianos,
delivering an odor of moths
to a slumbering attic.

    See how it drifts now,
leaving sparrow tracks
between phrases;
note its dry silence
and how it keeps itself
always what it is —
      perpetual chaff
      from crumbling grinders —

yet gives itself
to whatever holds still
or pauses,
asking nothing
except to draw its long sleeve
forever
over windows and highways
and the sleeping mouths
of lovers.

Riding Hood, Updated

There had to have been a wolf that night,
alive in his rank fur and throat,
ears twigged, wild feet leaving flowers
on spring-deep earth. The howl was there;
his shadow kept house behind every bush.

Remember, dead grandmother,
me in my hood, and the old rifle swinging
between us, ready for that hot tongue's flash?
There was a moon, too, skull-shaped but red.
Clouds leaned against it,
and the pines were windy harps.
A lake beckoned blue somewhere
like sky at the end of a downhill road.

There must have been an owl, as well,
feather-corseted, hinged with claws;
and a bobcat's cry.
Who knows what other things
lurked there?

It is nothing now to you
snug in your bonnet of earth,
out of the howl, forever wolf-free.
Here where the hunt goes on,
and unimaginable beasts are loose,
it's different for me.

Transition: New Mexico

There are winds here, too,
big-throated, sometimes with echoes
of the Pacific's blue yell and murmur:
at times a hint
of wet-weed-smell,
the spines of starfish stenciled in granite.

There is hail-flash here,
organs of thunder,
though rain is a thin flute.
Still, the hummingbird has come
to the feeder's glass flower,
and the sparrowhawk glistens on wires.
There are trees, as well —
huge harps or only dusty spinnets —
and clouds formal as monuments.

But ghosts hover in corners:
spectre of ocean,
wraith of gulls canting
over the white forest of the city
on the sail-boated bay.

I shall go out and walk in the desert.
I shall speak to the panting lizard
and touch (carefully)
the little bayonets of cacti.
I shall go to the racetrack
where the mountains lean
like giant, stone women.

I will learn to love the roadrunner
in his ungainly stride
as I once did the brown pelican

in the high-rise of sky
reflected in a room of tides.
I will make deliberate paths
through piñon dry as green cloth,
and over mesas composed of rock-rainbows,

but without sea salt to sting,
though there will be salt here,
of a kind,
as keen in the tooth and as blind
as all salt anywhere.

Space Probes

Our mechanical heroes have made their leap
and hunt among the cloven stars,
their metal foreheads tracking beeps
through wild menageries of space
and meteors shrill as an orchestra of keys.

There, once, plain gods with simple curls
bundled the air between their thighs
and rode in orbits of their will,
played common harps, invented skies,
and left upon the unrolled wind
long messages.
                    Those voices are still
unless the howl of things contains
a code designed for special ears —
as when on Earth a cold bush burned
like comet's hair, and called one man by name.

Rear Guard

Each year
we vow to leave these star-scorched firs
that in a thrashing wind
become brash lovers of our roof
and crash too near;
the fire of nettles, hornets, ticks;
the brittle seeds and bark
that litter the rain spout's narrow throat;
the skunk that performed a moonlit dance
upon our deck
but left its clinging stink.

Each year
we vow to find retreat
in some safe high-rise place
above a blaze of thoroughfares
and perfect parks.

Our daphne and quince are cropped by deer;
in our cupboards the flickering mice
cartwheel and nibble tomorrow's meal.
The melancholy owl, each night,
recites an elegy for whatever wildnesses
we try to keep.

Decision is not always deep,
sometimes affected by a simple shift of light,
a sudden leaf where no leaf had tried before,
or just an arrogant doe
who walked out of the woods one day
with her two fawns
to the birdbath.
They stared at us, then drank
without so much as asking us,

flickered their tails and left.

We stay
in rural danger, beauty, here,
protecting what remains.

Greenwich Mean Time **IV**

Solar Time

The time unit most commonly employed
since prehistoric times is the apparent daily circuit
of the sun.
  — Columbia Encyclopedia

The sun —
        that rolling hill of fire,
        that furnace hung past blistering ice —
                from it our ticking lives suspend:
                hearts, crops, and clocks,
                appointments, graduations, games;
                even the cricket
                with his bronze leather thighs
                leans on its soundless swing
                around our rooted world.

The sun —
        that fist of sparks,
        that furious star —
                on it the rattling mouse depends,
                the gull that seeks
                blue elevators in the wind,
                and the deep whale lounging
                in basements beyond light or sight
                but still hauled by the sun,
                and locked in time.

        Children regret the fever of its going,
        then race against insidious dusk
        to carry their lengthening shadows home.

                The cocktail hour diminishes and dies;
                a last lamp surrenders to the dark;
                and we, the daily circuit done,
                turn to the wall and strive again
                for the solstice of blind sleep.

Star Time

Khufu, builder of the Great Pyramid,
had a "telescope" installed within the walls.

The stone spy hole, lensless, immovable,
a stationary eye set in a tomb,
was aimed to catch the northern star
at its bright work — a seeming firefly
that moved mechanically as if on wires
some cunning engineer had strung
across the upsidedown abyss
of reachless sky.
                        Slaves snored beside
the salt-gray rocks their backs had hauled
through aisles of sweat; only a king had time
to gaze at splendid trinkets overhead:
blue chandeliers, red pendants, pearls,
a comet like a long-tailed, blazing fish.
Each night he knelt beneath his crown,
eyes pressed to that crude orifice,
his funeral chamber at his back.

On every cloudless watch, the star swung past
the dazzled aperture, its punctual glow
turning time into something measurable as light
though the room was black, as blood was black
when it darkened in the sand-pocked air
where workers burst their lungs and died.
The sepulchre at night was cool
and at the instant when the tail
of Ursa Minor flashed
above the limestone telescope
its ice glow made a sudden silver run
down royal hair and cheek and lip.
He felt the chill and prayed

to Osiris in whose hot loins
the sun's seeds rode.
                    The star steered on
and he was moved to think
what other power, when he was gone,
could put a similar will on space.

    His mummy sleeps, like some thick, paper worm.
    Even the eyes are gone
    that saw Polaris stride
    on its invisible stilts
    above that mammoth, pointed grave.
    Time, metered out, he found
    was less starlight than rot
    in spite of spices stuffed
    within the scooped-out cavity
    where once his lungs and liver toiled
    to keep his dreaming breath alive.

The heart, for all its lengthy bath
in priestly brines
became a thimbleful of air
not even archeologists can weigh.
There, as in lesser shrines,
only dust — some teeth —
some scraps of hair —
emit a starless gleam
beneath a finite flashlight's ray,
and heaven (all heavens anywhere)
remains light-years,
night-years, away.

Gregorian Adjustment, 1582

George Washington's birthday, February 11,
Old Style; February 22, New Style

The equinox was out of joint.
In twelve hundred years plus fifty-seven
the trusted calendar went awry,
developed an error of ten days,
so nothing matched.
Leaves bloomed too late;
birds nested in blank boughs;
even roosters were crowing out of tune.

Pope Gregory on his stiff throne
bent brow to fist,
attempting to reel time back
to something rational and true.
From prayer and thought he ruled
ten strumpet days must be tossed out
upon the dump heap of eternity,
the daily reckoning rectified.

Time is a racer and a sloth.
The Pope's chill bones
were tapestry
by the time his rectification came
to the American Colonies
and caught Ben Franklin
out of time . . .
ten days plus one
(a leap year's maverick sprint)
to be deducted from the total sum
of trips abroad, tomes, kites, and love.
Franklin was one who treasured sleep,
regreted those sweet hours lost;

yet philosophy with him ran deep,
and time was but a sieve, he knew,
through which one must expect a leak.

Our founding fathers took in stride
corrections of inevitable flaws.
Some losses had to be.
Birthdays were hustled into line,
adjustments made for wages lost,
new dates assigned to deaths or anniversaries.
But still the gap yawns there:
eleven days of expurgated history.

Indications of Time

Announcement of the sun
and birds quilting shadows
while the clock sits,
black hands folded;
recital of cars in hurried evening,
and a bull-horned moon
with a blue cape behind it;
pink and terror
of the day's shell-breaking,
and the thin thighs of crabs
designing the seashore;
sigh of the machine
with its iron pulse straining
and the nurse's wrench
seeking to soothe it;
thunder of the nerve
with its red tooth waking;
stillness of time
with two arms extended.
A bone sits on the clock
and the bone is ticking.

Midnight Saving Time

How to deal with these hours,
alone under the ceiling's black canopy
while the clock multiplies its two fingers
into ten, eleven, twelve,
cracks its knuckles at midnight,
builds an exclamation point,
then starts all over again?

My pillow smells of smoke,
skin lotions, gin, and something wilder,
almost out of time,
as when some other anxious head, on rock
or weeds, rolled in a vision
of a world being born
out of an animal stink and splendor;
invented an upright spine
and walked this way
and to this room
to stand in his primordial hair,
hand grasping mine.

Cousin, your cave was better than you knew.
Except for you, we might have stayed
beyond the mind's chill blast,
the wheel's hot, greasy stride,
scratching our fleas
but wrapped in snores
beside a warm, exhausted mate,
our only clock a waterfall or gonging moon.

I await, awake, the gadgetries of day —
the percolator plugged into my veins,
the toaster clicking with my borrowed nerves,
and then the traffic's grinding games,

my blood a pawn, all hours blown
down office shafts and streets and bars
until, again, the pitch and pall of night.

You with your shaggy eye and reach
would have saved at least some bone from these.
I munch on air, not knowing how to use
either my darkness or my light.

Lifetime

I am at the age when you grow ten years older
in one year . . .
   — Ionesco

The slowing down, the lag and the slack
on common stairs and hills, are all external
like warts that blossom overnight
in the mirror, and the white wires that sprout
from nostril and eyebrow. Within,
dark within the coverings of skin and cloth,
deep within the trappings of bone and blood,
there is a runner racing ever faster
to gain a leap on the lip of the grin
where the world slips, slides, ends.

How nimble the inward chase,
how ardent the gray-haired sprinter
though he stumble over a thread
or have hands as unsteady as water;
how yet he pursues the instant of breath
between the cry into light
and the cry into darkness,
and the time-stop machine always ticking.

The past is my runner's cape.
It flows out behind me like a train
of dust —
        though there are sparks in it
burning with rubies and roses,
flash of warm arms, great moons rising,
scent of grass gathered into green curtains,
mirages of mouths, eyes, swimmers, sleepers,
fragrance of voices,
memories of lust satisfied
(lovely as the wind's firelight on mountains),

but all of it a streaming trail of dust
blown backward as I race ever faster —
how the dawns rush by me —
to escape my own hunting shadow.

Dateline: Calendar Time

The day begins with an imaginary line
drawn over the Pacific's tilt and boom,
invisible thread that knots the sun,
gossamer hurdle for flying fish,
unseen barrier through which ships pass
as through a horizontal ghost.

No ruler drew the dateline's rigid spine
across tumultuous earth and wave
except the ruler of the mind
with its lean edge.
Inflexible, imperious, it makes a boundary
between midnight and dawn,
governs the submarine's wet glide,
the airliner's takeoff and speed,
all trains, all barges, subways, cars,
and regulates the garbage truck's
arrival in a brittle street
where sleepers deep in inner rooms
pace their own dreams by that thin strand.

But breath-time, heart-time, circadian,
is finer than a dotted line.
Stretched taut on hemispheres within,
it knows precisely when the sun
swims into night, and how,
some hour, it will never rise again
in spite of travelers' clocks
or planes, or dolphins rainbowing across
a frail, fictitious wake
of what seems something like a dawn
but is in fact eternal dark.

Round-Trip Passenger: Jet Time

No journey is to be undertaken lightly
whether over mountains, through meadows,
or into a tunnel that like a rifle barrel
has a distant, flickering eye of blue;
all can become, in an instant, fire.

Nor is the pattern always true
between one horizon and another,
the aim seldom being steady
but a conjunction of ascent and falling,
of unforeseen stars that must be followed,
of trestles broken, the train still howling onward;
or ships, even canoes, with a hidden fault —
some rivet askew, or only rot working
with its unheard singsong of patience.

For those on wings, the hazard is highest.
Time, where the keen jets scorch the sky,
whirls out of place, spins on its hub,
reels back, ahead, squats in a trance
until no passenger can trust his watch
or stammering pulse to know the hour.
Even the terminal clock can seem a liar
to travelers descending out of clouds —
those round, white blossomers,
those orchards drifting beyond touch
above fields copied, and revised,
from textbooks on geometry, the pages green,
or deserts spread like lion skins
between the wrinkled maps of streams.

To arrive at last, to take the risk
of stepping down from sunrise into dark
(since back where you took flight for home

dawn held its yellow sparkler up —
and there were passionate promises,
already lies though bold as the rifle's stare),
then to haul the midnight baggage out
from that time zone to this
and wade on jet-lag thighs
a ramp familiar as breath
but changed — steeper and narrower than you knew —
and suddenly perilous.

Greenwich Mean Time

Begin with zero here on this low hill
where the Thames, broad-backed and brown
ferries its load of yachts and excrement
past the invisible but Prime Meridian,
that hatchery in which time spawns
swift minnow seconds fattening in a leap
toward minutes, hours, years,
a century, millenium, eternity.

The monster has a voice like a tin bird
clucking across the short-wave band.
It chirps, it cheeps, it keens
out of the plastic cage that amplifies
the smallest whisper the transmitter makes;
invades the bedroom, closet, bath,
the lisping church, the conference room.
A human ventriloquist speaks for it:
"At the sound of the tone
it will be five hours . . ." (six? twelve? none?)
"four minutes, Greenwich Mean Time."

Begin with zero where
the red-faced infant yowls at birth;
the mausoleum perches with its crypt;
the bombers dive and drop their howling loads
to deliver the final cipher, death;
and here, within this interval,
where all of us (hearing the countdown
from every screen) seek ways, meantime,
to live within our limited means.

Beyond Greenwich

I am going to go down into the tides
where the moon swings
and time is as dark as the shark's fin
wrinkling above a white spool of water.
I am going to learn
from the cold tunes of congers
what ocean time is
and how it booms over
the announcement of bells
on a liner's deck.

I shall plunge through
the green gut of the abyss,
far below serpent or urchin,
down where blackness and silence
make midnight seem a blaze of operas.

I shall dive deep, deeper.
I shall become a fish of sorts.
I shall wear a skin of icicles.
I shall avoid all hooks
though my teeth be as sharp
as the cutting edge of the wings of swans.

Acknowledgments

The following poems, a number of them revised, are reprinted by permission of the periodicals and anthologies in which they first appeared: From *The Christian Century*, "Explorers, One, Two, Three, Etc.," now "Space Probes." From *Epoch*, "Landscape," now "Waste," and "The Sleep of Animals." From *Hearse*, "Stop Watch," now "True Crime." From *Kayak*, "Deluge," "Fashion Model at Home," "Indications of Time," "This Being the Evening," and "The Brotherhood." From *The Mississippi Review*, "Dust." From *The Nation*, "From the Diggings." From *Pebble*, "Drumcliffe: Passing By" and "Tulip Fancier." From *Poetry Northwest*, "As It Is," "Self-Portrait," "Cellar," "The Watch," now "Hypochondria," "A Winter View," "Message," "Midnight Saving Time," "Lifetime," "Anywhere," "Structures," and "Summer." From *Poetry NOW*, "Solo, Non-Stop," "Conflagrations," "Judgment Day," and "Rest Home." From *Prairie Schooner*, "Iowa Biography," copyright 1974 by the University of Nebraska Press. From *Road Apple Review*, "Art Colony by the Sea." From *Seven Poets* (Best Cellar Press, special *Pebble* #16, 1977), "Dogskin Rug" and "Solar Time." From *The Southern Poetry Review*, "After Provincetown," now "Shore Leave: Provincetown." From *Steppenwolf*, "f/16, 1/500." From *The Sunstone Review*, "Transition: New Mexico." From *The Western Humanities Review*, "Ivory Paper Weight" and "Whales." From *Works*, "Passenger: Jet Time," now "Round-trip Passenger: Jet Time," and "San Andreas City: For Active Adults." From *Yankee*, "Country School" and "Water Strider." From *Yes: A Magazine of Poetry*, "Stopover: Iceland," "V.D. Clinic," "Night Cabin," and "Point of View."

Adrien Stoutenburg

Adrien Stoutenburg was born in Minnesota but has lived in
California for much of her life, with shorter stays in Santa Fe
and Denver. She has worked at various times as a political
reporter and a country librarian, and she was an editor for
Parnassus Press in Berkeley. Her longest career has been in
children's literature, with thirty-five published books for young
readers, including one volume of poems, *The Things That Are*.

Stoutenburg has published two other collections of poetry,
Heroes, Advise Us, winner of the Academy of American Poets
Lamont Poetry Award, and *Short History of the Fur Trade*,
winner of the California Commonwealth Club Award for Poetry.
Her poetry is widely published in anthologies and periodicals
such as *The New Yorker* and *The Saturday Review*. Winner of
two Poetry Society of America awards, she is also co-winner
of the *Poetry Northwest* Helen Bullis Award and winner of
nine Borestone Mountain poetry awards.